4TH GRADE HISTORY BOOK: MAYANS AND INCAS OF SOUTH AMERICA

SPEEDY
PUBLISHING

Speedy Publishing LLC
40 E. Main St. #1156
Newark, DE 19711
www.speedypublishing.com

The two most dominant and advanced civilizations that developed in the Americas were the Maya, and the Inca.

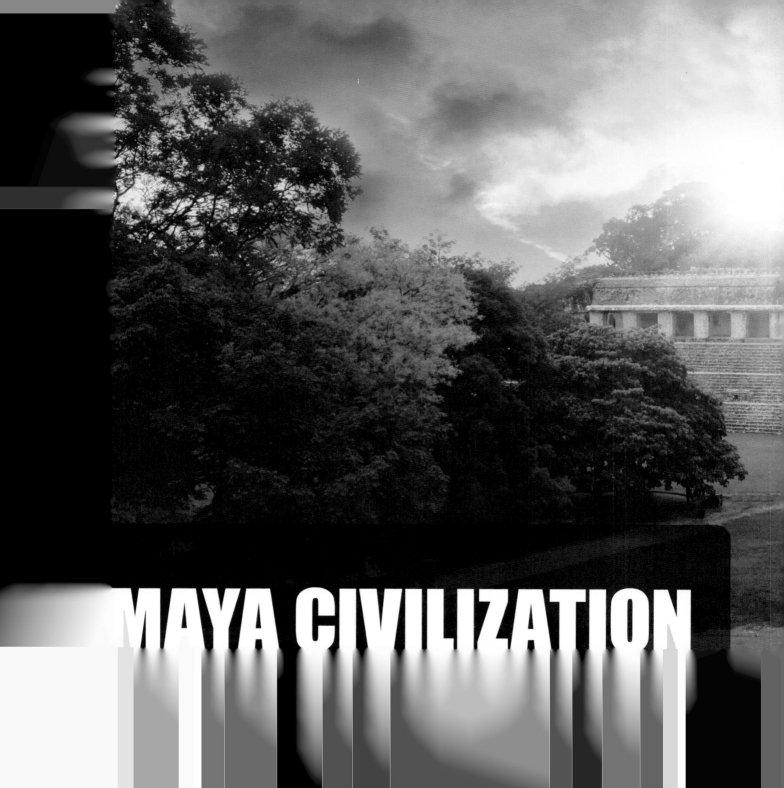

MAYA CIVILIZATION

The Ancient Mayan lived in the Yucatán around 2600 B.C. Today, this area is southern Mexico, Guatemala, northern Belize and western Honduras.

The position of king was usually inherited by the oldest son. If there wasn't a son then the oldest brother became king.

The Maya considered crossed eyes, flat foreheads, and big noses to be beautiful features. They would use makeup to try and make their noses appear large.

INCA EMPIRE

The Inca Empire existed in Peru. The Empire had ruled much of the region since the early 1400s.

The Inca Empire had large stone cities, beautiful temples, an advanced government, a detailed tax system, and a road system.

Many people had to pay their taxes through labor. They worked for the government as soldiers, builders, or farmers in order to pay their taxes.

Printed in Great Britain
by Amazon

Published by
Speedy Publishing LLC
40 E. Main St., #1156
Newark DE 19711

Cover by 24HR Covers

ISBN 978-1-68260-175-

THE NOGRE

by DICK CLEMENT

Illustrations by Christopher Whittle